DIRECTING PUPPET THEATRE

Carol Fijan and Frank Ballard
with Christina Starobin

RESOURCE PUBLICATIONS, INC. • San Jose, California

Editorial director: Kenneth Guentert
Production editor: Elizabeth J. Asborno
Art director: Ron Niewald
Cover design and production/Mechanical pasteup: Andrew Wong
Photographs (except where otherwise noted): National Theatre of Puppet
   Arts, Inc. (Great Neck, New York)
Diagram illustrations: David Ballard
Photo of Frank Ballard, back cover: Laramie Photography
Photo of Christina Starobin, back cover: Cara Lise Metz

Library of Congress Cataloging in Publication Data

Fijan, Carol.
    Directing puppet theatre step by step / by Carol Fijan
    and Frank Ballard ; text by Christina Starobin.
        p.   cm.
    Bibliography: p.
    ISBN 0-89390-126-1
    1. Puppets and puppet-plays. I. Ballard, Frank, 1929-
    II. Starobin, Christina, 1949-   . III. Title.
    PN1972.F524 1989
    791.5'3dc19

                                                    88-35659
5 4 3 2
93 92 91 90

To Kathy Kane, whose criticisms, comments, advice, and encouragement made this book possible.

Contents

Diagrams

Acknowledgments

The authors gratefully acknowledge the contribution of colleagues and friends in making this book possible.

To Dr. Herman Starobin for his help in editing the text and to Ms. Adah Ruth Ballard for her patience and encouragement.

To Pat Lay Wilson for compiling the bibliography.

Special thanks to Dr. Leo Gross, Janet Andriano, Hilary Boal, George Bouza, Louis Decker, E. Marie Doran, Pamela Friedman, Mark Gardner, Angela Glueckert, Larry Kurtzberg, Estelle Laster, James Leonard III, Carol E. Levy, Elizabeth Nelson, Elizabeth Paturzo, Ruth Swan, Shirley Roman, Paul Vincent-Davis, and our two young puppeteers, Lily Gross and Sosh Andriano, and Joseph Good, for his counsel.

And last, but far from least, to William Burns, our publisher, who recognized the need for this book.

Introduction

This book is intended for puppet groups both large and small—from the one-person show to large groups; for amateurs, semi-professionals, and professionals. It is also meant for community groups, scout groups, schools, libraries, churches, and special education groups (handicapped, emotionally disturbed, deaf, English as a Second Language, and so on). We seek to provide a solid background in directing, resulting in a show that will delight both performers and their audiences.

Even when one has mastered the technical skills needed to bring a puppet to life, chosen a script, and made the puppets and scenery, the play still requires a director. In fact, the director should be there at the beginning of the production to coordinate all efforts and to give the play its fundamental unity. After reading these pages, the reasons for these assertions will be clear.

This book's systematic approach leads to an understanding of why certain directing principles are valid and explains how to apply these principles to actual situations. It is one of the first coordinated studies on the subject.

We seek to cover the varied aspects of directing puppet productions. Groups will be able to use the material presented to organize their own approach. Puppeteers who wish to become directors will be able to increase their knowledge. We also hope to provide guidance for groups whose budgets do not allow for a full-time director.

The experiences of the authors in teaching puppetry and directing puppet productions have helped to refine the basic points presented so that they may be easily understood and put into practice. Amply illustrated with photographs, charts, and diagrams, the examples given in each chapter aim to take this book off the shelf and put it into the hands of the director, where it can function as a tool for a successful performance.

This book is the combined effort of Carol Fijan and Frank Ballard. Carol is co-author of *Making Puppets Come Alive* (Taplinger Publishing Company, 1973), director of the award-winning Teen Concert Theatre, and founder and director of the National Theatre of Puppet Arts, Inc. Frank is professor of dramatic arts at the University of Connecticut and a past president of Puppeteers of America and UNIMA-USA (Union International de la Marionnette). The text is written by Christina Starobin, international award-winning poet, writer, and puppeteer.

Chapter

1

The Group

A puppet group may vary in size from one to twenty-five or more people. Its members may be students, amateurs, semi-professionals, or professionals. The age group can range anywhere from first graders to senior citizens. The groups can be a part of the school system or university, or sponsored by the community, a local library, arts center, boy or girl scout troup, church, or any other organization. All puppet groups, however, have at least one thing in common: They must have a director.

The director coordinates all the efforts that go into a production and is the leader of the group.

Experience teaches that to make group organizations more effective, the following functions must also be filled: a secretary, a treasurer, someone responsible for publicity pictures and brochures, and if the group travels, someone to make the necessary arrangements.

Chapter

Responsibilities of a Director

Webster's Third New International Dictionary tells us that a director is "one that supervises the production of a show...with responsibility for action, lighting, music, rehearsals, and generally for giving substance to the conception of the author."

Therefore, even before work on a play commences, you, the director, must visualize the production in its entirety and come to the group completely prepared. These abilities constitute the unique quality of a good director.

As in all forms of theatre, the puppet director should not be a member of the cast. This frees you to observe and guide the production from the point of view of the audience.

As a director in a puppet group, you have a number of key tasks. You are responsible for the group and must see that the members give the best performance possible. You give guidance to the individual group members and tie up all the loose ends in a production. You have the final say in all matters.

You must, of course, be familiar with the art of puppetry and know the various types of puppets—hand, rod,

Front view of a hand and rod puppet. From the play *Kismet*, University of Connecticut, directed by Frank Ballard. Design by Frank Ballard.

Back view of hand and rod puppet, showing the puppeteers' hands.

mouth, marionette, shadow, or combinations—and what each type can and cannot do. You should decide which kind of puppet is most appropriate for the production.

LEADERSHIP AND CRITIQUE

As a group leader, you should know how to deal with the people in the group, whether they are children or adults, and respect and value their opinions. You must also know just how much weight to place on such opinions and be as objective as possible. Only by striving for objectivity will a director's opinions have

validity.

These leadership qualities will be most evident when you offer criticism to group members. Criticism should be positive. First say what is specifically good in a performance and then what can be done to im-

Front view of hand puppets. TV pilot, "The Glovekins," National Puppet Associates. Design by Maury Haykin.

Front view of hand puppets, showing the puppeteers' hands inside the puppets and holding props.

Back view of "Bunraku"-type puppet, showing puppeteers.

prove the puppeteer's work. By calling attention to what can be done to correct or improve the performance, criticism serves a positive function. Such criticism tends to eliminate pettiness and helps the one giving the critique to analyze constructively what can be done to improve the production.

A good director asks for the opinions of the group members in critique sessions as part of getting them involved in all aspects of the production. This gives them the opportunity to improve their own leadership abilities and contributes to the creative process of the production.

A good sense of organization is essential. If the puppet group is part of the school system, you should be aware of

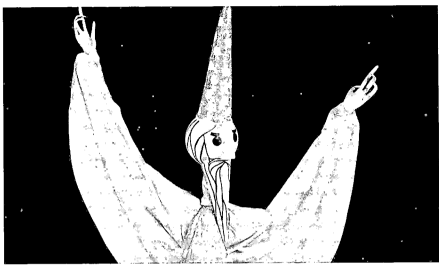

Front view of full-size "Bunraku"-type puppet. *The Sorcerer's Den*, Teen Concert Theatre (Great Neck, NY). Design by Paul Vincent-Davis; costume by Carol Fijan.

advantages that may exist. It may be possible to call upon specialists for assistance. The art department can design costumes, puppets, and scenery. The shop program can construct the stage or heavier scenery. The music department may suggest background music or may even compose original themes. The bus company that services the school can help with travel arrangements.

If the group is part of a library or is community sponsored, it may be possible to ask parents for help. A parent can volunteer to serve as group secretary. Another parent may secure at wholesale certain materials needed to make puppets or scenery. Parents often enjoy such involvement.

Front view of marionette showing puppeteer manipulating strings. From *Two By Two*, University of Connecticut. Design by Frank Ballard.

Side view of marionette and puppeteer.

FINANCES

If you are lucky enough to have someone to handle the financial aspects of the production, your job will be considerably easier. If not, you will have to consider how much money is available for a production and how it will be used. This aspect of the production should be discussed at business meetings, which, depending upon the size and makeup of the group, may be combined with rehearsals.

If a group is fortunate enough to have a large budget, jobs such as stage manager, tour manager, etc., can be allocated. If not, you must assume these roles.

You must also remember to figure into the budget the cost

Close-up front view of glove puppets, showing the puppeteers' hands. *Show of Hands*, National Puppet Associates. Design by Shirley Roman.

Front view of glove puppets, showing the puppeteers' hands.

of materials for the puppets, costumes, props, scenery, and sound. Other costs may include printing tickets, leaflets, and posters, and buying penny-saver ads or radio or television spots. Records of cash flow should be kept so that no questions arise that cannot be checked quickly.

You must be prepared to make decisions with which the group may disagree. You should remember, however, that any hostility that develops usually disappears with the curtain calls and the cast party.

Front view of mouth puppet made from two boxes. Class exercise, North Shore Community Art Center (Great Neck, NY). Design by a student, age ten.

Inside view of mouth puppet, showing the puppeteer's hand.

9

TOP: Front view of stick puppets. Class exercise, North Shore Community Art Center (Great Neck, NY). Design by a student, age eight.

MIDDLE: Front view of stick puppets, showing hands holding sticks. .

BOTTOM: Front view of finger puppets. TV pilot, "The Glovekins," National Puppet Associates. Design by Carol Fijan.

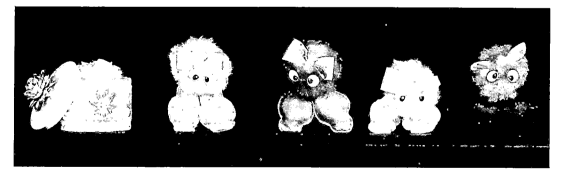

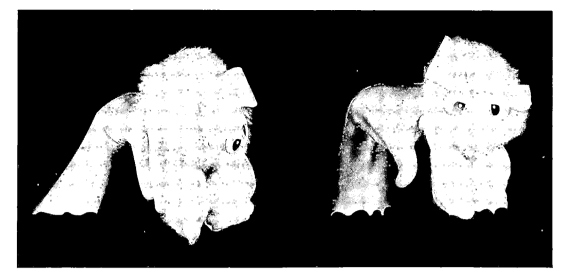

TOP: Side view of finger puppets, showing puppeteer's hands.

RIGHT: Front view of full-size puppet with mask head. *Love for Three Oranges,* directed by Frank Ballard, University of Connecticut. Design b Frank Ballard.

BOTTOM: Back view of "mask" puppet, showing puppeteer.

Front view of shadow puppets. *Rumpelstiltskin*, National Puppet Associates. Design by Marjorie Shanafelt.

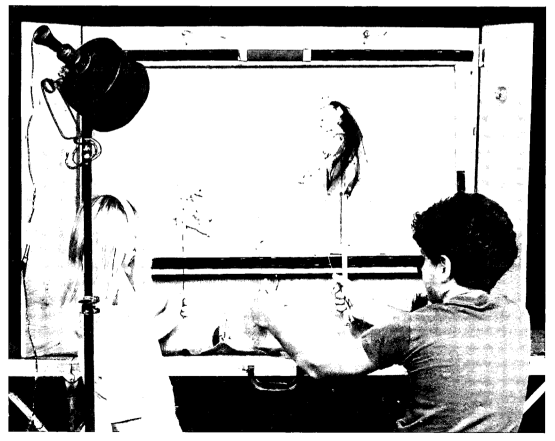

Back view of shadow puppets, showing shadow screen and puppeteers.

Chapter

3

The Script

WHO, WHAT, AND WHERE

In supervising the choice of a script, you must first consider the audience. Is it composed of children or adults? If it is children, are they of various ages? Is it a nightclub audience? Is it a special audience—for example, a national group or the handicapped? Is the performance for a health program such as

Examples of puppets used in scripts derived from Aesop's Fables. *The Lion and the Mouse*, Kathy Kane Puppets. Design by Kathy Kane.

one about drug and alcohol abuse? Is it for the inmates of a correctional facility?

Next, you must consider the performing group. Is it composed of individuals without a great deal of experience in the art of puppetry; is it a mature group with training; is it one that has been together for a long time?

The suitability of the script to the type of puppets is another consideration. Combinations of types of puppets can also be used in a production.

When is the show to be presented? Is it a seasonal show such as a Christmas production, or is it one that can be performed year-round?

Where is the show to be performed? Will it be played in the same place, or will it tour?

Examples of puppets used in scripts derived from fairy tales. *Little Red Riding Hood*, National Puppet Productions. Design by Paul Vincent-Davis and Carol Fijan.

SOURCES FOR SCRIPTS

Keeping these elements in mind, begin to search for a script. The ideal script is one written especially for the group or one composed from the group's own improvisations. Libraries also have many books of puppet plays, if time or other factors prevent writing an original script.

Good sources for script ideas can be found in fairy tales, folklore, Aesop's fables, mythology, legends, and the Bible. Such well-known stories as *Heidi, Treasure Island, Alice in Wonderland,* or the stories of Rudyard Kipling or A. A. Milne provide good material for scripts.

Cartoons are also a valuable source of material for a puppet

Examples of puppets used in scripts derived from nursery rhymes. *The Three Little Kittens*, North Shore Community Arts Center. (Great Neck, NY). Design by student, age ten.

Examples of puppets used in scripts derived from poetry. *The Owl and the Pussycat*, North Shore Community Arts Center (Great Neck, NY). Design by student, age ten.

Examples of puppets used in scripts derived from folk tales, stories, ballads, etc., of many lands and people. Japanese folk tale, National Puppet Productions. Design by Paul Vincent-Davis.

Examples of puppets used in scripts derived from the Bible. *Adventures on Noah's Ark,* National Puppet Associates. Design by Shirley Roman.

play, as are many other forms of satire.

Why not use a conventional theatrical script? This idea frequently comes to mind and is not necessarily a bad one. But in adapting theatre scripts, certain critical aspects must be recognized: puppetry is basically a pantomime art form. It is visual. Its basis is in movement. Conventional theatre, on the other hand, is written to be heard. A script for actors may have long speeches that will not play well with puppets. Puppet scripts need short lines to emphasize the interplay between characters. Complex dialogue does not work well, either.

Puppets are not little people or little animals. They are the essence of a person or of a feeling. If they talk too much, one becomes aware of their artificiality. When doing a theatrical script with puppets, one should ask, "Why use puppets?" There should be a specific reason for using puppets. They should enhance the script, but they are not a substitute for people.

If you choose to adapt a theatrical script, you should edit it judiciously. Possible copyright problems should also be investigated before going

Examples of puppets used in scripts derived from Greek and Roman mythology. *Prometheus Bound*, National Theatre of Puppet Arts, Inc. (Great Neck, NY). Design by Paul Vincent-Davis; costume by Carol Fijan.

Examples of puppets used in scripts derived from science fiction. *Outer-Space*, Repertory Puppet Company (Washington, D.C.). Design by Paul Vincent-Davis.

17

Examples of puppets used in scripts derived from current events. *Show of Hands*, National Puppet Associates. Design by Carol Fijan.

Examples of puppets used in scripts derived from original stories on original themes. *The Adventures of Wee and Uss and the Buried Treasure*, National Puppet Associates. Design by Carol Fijan and Shirley Roman.

into production.

If choosing a musical or an opera, there are additional problems. Because there is little or no variation in the facial expression of puppets, songs may easily become boring and artificial.

As with any rule, there are exceptions. The classics are one branch of theatre that can be successfully performed by puppets. A director can edit the classics with no copyright problems.

Shakespeare can also be done to advantage. The sleepwalking scene from *Macbeth*, for example, combines relatively short speeches with movements that are the focus of the action. If working with Shakespeare, a certain amount of editing is necessary. You should try to get the help of a Shakespearean scholar.

Theatre of the Absurd can also be performed by puppets because it deals in concepts that are already abstract. The frequent use of pantomime and stylization is most suitable for puppetry.

If you are fortunate enough to have an original script written for the group, you should make certain that the writer is aware of the strengths and limitations of puppets.

Some of the finest scripts come from group improvisational material.

Instead of one play, a group may decide to combine several short plays with a common theme. A group of fables can be presented as a unity. A literary or philosophical theme may be chosen, such as "lovers through the ages."

Once the script is chosen, some preliminary decisions must be made. How many people are in the group? If the group is large, you may need to add extra characters to the script. If the group is small, you may have to reduce the number of characters in the play.

A production does not have to look like conventional theatre. It is perfectly acceptable to use puppets that are abstract forms. Music and poetry are especially suited to presentations with abstract forms. And since any object brought to life by a human being is a puppet, the source of materials upon which to base the production is limitless.

HOW TO WRITE DIALOGUE

In adapting a well-known story, *Cinderella* for example, you should ask, "How do I get the actual script, the actual

Examples of puppets used in scripts derived from musical tone poems. *Carnival of the Animals* by Saint-Saens, University of Connecticut. Design by Frank Ballard.

Examples of puppets used in scripts derived from Shakespeare. *Excerpts from Shakespeare*, National Theatre of Puppet Arts (Great Neck, NY). Design by Shirley Roman; costume by Carol Fijan.

19

Examples of puppets used in scripts derived from the opera. Mozart's *The Magic Flute*, University of Connecticut, directed by Frank Ballard. Design by Frank Ballard. (Photo by Richard Termine.)

dialogue, for the story?" There are many ways. The following is one of the most successful, used by the University of Connecticut puppet program and by the North Shore Community Arts Center puppet students.

The scene is from *Where Are You, Cinderella*, in which the Fairy Godmother appears and prepares Cinderella for the ball.

Divide the group into units of two. In each twosome, let the members decide who will play Cinderella and who will play the Fairy Godmother. Then direct the group members to talk to each other in their respective roles. Let all the twosomes do this at the same time. It will sound like bedlam as they improvise the scene. Each pair then performs its improvisation for the entire company.

You can either videotape the improvisations or take notes on the best improvised dialogue. The best lines may then be used as the basis for the script. Do this for as much of the script as possible. In this way, each group member has a chance to play every part and to add his or her ideas to the script.

Do not be afraid to cut lines. You should get the dialogue down to the absolute minimum. Dialogue has only one purpose: to further the plot. A word or sentence that does not further the plot should be cut.

When the script is ready, your responsibility is to bring the product to life. The mood, the music and sound, the design of the puppets, the scenery and props, and the color coordination all flow from the central concept of the script.

Chapter

4

Analyzing the Script: The Approach

To lead the group effectively, you must know the script thoroughly. The more you analyze the script in detail and with care, the easier it will be to direct the production.

A play is usually written with a beginning, middle, and end. These divisions are known as "acts." The first act introduces the characters and the conflict. The second develops the plot and deepens characterizations. The third act resolves the conflict.

In addition to this preliminary rule of thumb, you should analyze the script according to the following nine subdivisions.

Purpose. All dialogue, movement, action, and characterization must have a purpose and must be justified in terms of what the play is saying. This purpose must be constantly in your mind.

Everything done should move the production forward and justify the message of the script. Each time a puppet moves, ask, "Is there a purpose to this movement? Does it just fill in time? Or is it there because we cannot think of anything else to do at this point?"

Placement. You must visualize everything in the production as a whole. First consider the points of the characters' entrance and exits. These may be doors, curtains, or just the place on stage where the puppets appear or disappear. The objective of such visualization is very important. You are creating a world larger than the one the audience sees on stage. The puppets must carry the audience's imagination

If there is no scenery and the puppets enter on the stage at a certain point, make them exit at the same point or the illusion of a specific entrance to the room will be lost.

beyond what is immediately visible.

Blocking. Blocking is the *who, when, what, where, why,* and *how* of putting together a puppet production. It is your way of establishing a pattern of movement and stage action for the puppet that will best convey

to the audience the character and the plot situation.

Use the script to plan the blocking of the production. The script may read, "Cinderella's sisters enter calling for Cinderella." What the director must establish is from *where* the sisters are coming, *how* they come in, *what* they do after they come in, and *what* their mood is. *Where* is Cinderella? Is she already on stage? If so, *where* is she, and *what* is she doing?

Four elements help you in blocking: positioning, picturization, movement, and rhythm.

Positioning. The stage is divided into various acting areas (Diagram 1). Positioning

UR	URC	UC	ULC	UL
R	RC	C	LC	L
DR	DRC	DC	DLC	DL

Diagram 1: Areas of the stage

Four positions in relation to stage and audience: (l to r) front, profile, 3/4 turn, and back. Design by Carol Fijan.

deals firstly with the location of a puppet within these acting areas. Secondly, positioning deals with the body positions of the puppet in relation to the audience.

Positioning is used to give focus. For example, usually a puppet that is speaking should be emphasized. One way of emphasizing this puppet is by placing it in a strong acting area. If this character is facing front, it is emphasized over other puppets that are placed in profile or three-quarter-turn positions. A puppet becomes important if it is elevated, while other characters are lowered.

Picturization. Picturization means exactly what the word implies: What does the picture created on the stage look like? You must constantly be aware that each changing stage picture conveys to the audience a new statement of mood and meaning. Eliminate anything that intrudes upon or distracts from the stage picture. Is a

Emphasized position by contrast with space. Design by Carol Fijan.

LEFT: Emphasized position by focus of other puppets. Design by Carol Fijan.

RIGHT: Emphasized position by elevation. Design by Carol Fijan.

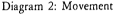

Diagram 2: Movement

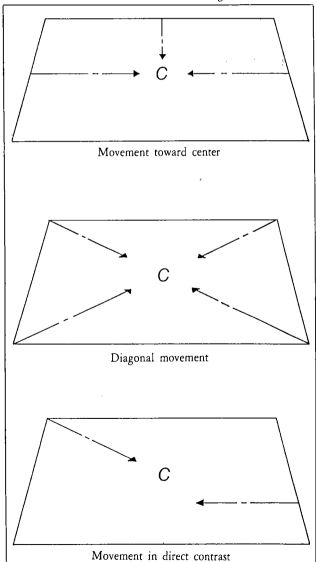

Movement toward center

Diagonal movement

Movement in direct contrast

puppeteer's hand visible? If the puppeteers are playing in view of the audience, is their costuming distracting? Does the proscenium overwhelm the production?

Movement. Movement is the stage picture in motion. A movement of the puppet toward center stage is strong. A diagonal movement is more forceful than a straight movement. A movement that is in direct contrast to other movements taking place simultaneously is also strong (Diagram 2.)

Rhythm. Each character has its own rhythm. The rhythmic pattern of a character is determined by the age, sex, ethnic background, position in life,

Rhythm of the hare. *Fables Are Forever*, National Puppet Productions. Design by Paul Vincent-Davis; costume by Carol Fijan.

Rhythm of the tortoise. *Fables Are Forever*, National Puppet Productions. Design by Paul Vincent-Davis; costume by Carol Fijan.

and education of the puppet. Younger characters have a freer, lighter rhythm than older characters. Animal characters have their own distinctive rhythm. A tortoise, for example, has its own rhythm, as does a rabbit.

Rhythm should not be confused with tempo. Tempo simply means faster or slower.

Rhythm in music is established by a specific beat to the measure. Drama also has its rhythms. The specific beat in drama is established by the dialogue, style (comedy, farce, or tragedy), and the physical change of the set and lights. Rhythm can be used to create the atmosphere and the locale where the play takes place. For example, the rhythm of the Caribbean islands is different than the rhythm of the Arctic.

Sometimes rhythm will vary from performance to performance, depending upon whether the puppeteers are tired, depressed, or even happy. Their moods will reflect their own personal rhythms, and these may not coincide with the rhythm of the performance. Sometimes there is a problem for the company that has taped its own show. The tape retains its own rhythm, energy level, and tempo, but the live movements of the puppeteers will differ depending upon how they feel while performing.

The rhythm of a scene can be destroyed by technical accidents over which you have no control. To mention a few: steam pipes knocking, the stage floor squeaking, or debris falling.

Phrasing. A play is broken into acts, which are divided into scenes; each scene is broken into smaller units called "French scenes." A French scene is the sequence of events that take place between the entrance and exit of a character.

Each French scene may be given a general description that has to do with its function, such as "the hero's declaration of love," "the agony of failure in battle," or "the dragon is slain and the hero is victorious." It is best to keep the number of French scenes to a minimum without leaving out any significant action.

Each French scene can be further separated into *phrases*. These phrases may be based on dialogue, on music, or on silence. Each phrase must move the scene closer to its ending

Common backstage noises that destroy the rhythm of the scene are the sound of the puppeteer's footsteps and the picking up and laying down of puppets and props. To avoid these distractions, puppeteers should work in stocking feet and pad the surfaces on which the puppets and props are placed.

and advance the purpose of the play.

For example, take the first half of the French scene in *Where Are You Cinderella?* (Act I, Scene 3). Her sisters have left for the ball. In our version, this scene takes place in the garden. The phrases are as follows:

phrase	1	Cinderella is sitting in the garden
phrase	2	Bird flies from corn stalk
phrase	3	Cinderella and bird come together
phrase	4	*flash of light*
phrase	5	Bird flies back to corn stalk
phrase	6	Cinderella jumps up
phrase	7	Fairy Godmother materializes
phrase	8	Cinderella freezes
phrase	9	Fairy Godmother moves toward Cinderella
phrase	10	Cinderella moves toward Fairy Godmother and asks,

"Who are you? Where did you come from?"

phrase 11   Fairy Godmother answers, "I am your Fairy Godmother."

phrase 12   Fairy Godmother waves wand and stalk becomes a flower

phrase 13   Cinderella runs toward Fairy Godmother and kneels before her

Patterns of the Phrases. Phrases have patterns that can be graphed. A soft and quiet phrase may be a curved line. A phrase with conflict can be an angular line with exaggerated highs and lows. A burst of light may have a distinctive pattern, as would crying. A graph is useful to depict the tempo of the scene (Diagram 3).

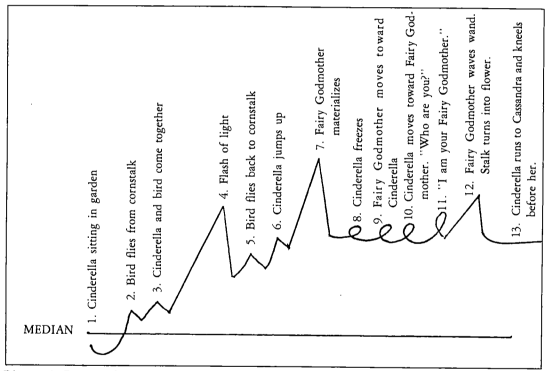

Diagram 3: Patterns of phrases

Tempo (Pacing) and Pause. Tempo follows directly from the patterns of the phrases. If we graph a scene and it has a regularly repeating curved line above the median, the whole scene will have a very slow tempo. If the graph is a line going up and down across the median, the scene will have a very fast tempo.

Tempo can be changed for a variety of reasons. For example, if the scene with Cinderella in the garden were at the beginning of the play, it might play better with a regular tempo. If it were in the middle of the play and the audience knew who the Fairy Godmother was but Cinderella did not, suspense can be built by slowing each phrase and changing its pattern and tempo. The same scene at the end of the play can be hurried if one wants a fast conclusion. One of the main flaws in many productions is that the tempo is not varied enough.

Tempo can be varied by the tone of voice and movement of the characters, or it can be varied by lighting changes. A scene lit by quiet, dim lights that suddenly switch to spots of moving lights and color will create a change of tempo.

Speech patterns vary the tempo automatically. Old people talk more slowly; younger people talk faster. The speech in a love scene may be sweet and slow. An angry scene or one with witches may be loud and fast.

Changing the scenery in full view of the audience can also help to vary the tempo. For example, by having the puppeteers change the scenery to accompanying music, the National Theatre of Puppet Art's production of *Excerpts from Shakespeare* modulated the change in mood and tempo from *Macbeth* to *Taming of the Shrew*.

A pause can also vary the tempo. The pause is the absence of sound and movement. It's purpose is to focus the audience's attention, give it time to react, build suspense, or highlight any significant moment. In puppetry this pause is called a *freeze*.

Use of the pause can be a very effective dramatic device. Recall the pause before Hamlet speaks to the skull as he holds it in his hand and gazes at it, or the pause at the end of the second act of *Madame Butterfly*, when evening falls as the characters wait for Pinkerton's return.

The use of the pause in comedy is a vital part of timing. There is the familiar pause in the comic chase when the two characters accidentally come face to face. The double take is one of the most familiar comic pauses. Use the pause sparingly, however. Be sure that it intensifies the action. A mistimed pause might make the audience think that a puppeteer has forgotten his or her lines.

Pantomime. Pantomime is the basis of all puppetry. It is the visual development of the story without words. A person whose hearing is impaired should be able to watch a puppet performance and understand the story because the movements the puppets make, the positions they assume, and their relationship to the stage are all clear and concise.

If words are necessary to explain the action, something is wrong with the blocking. If it hasn't been said in pantomime, it hasn't been said. Too many puppeteers rely on dialogue to tell the story when it should be apparent from watching the pantomime.

For example, the previous garden scene from *"Where Are You, Cinderella?"* had on-

To avoid unnecessary dialogue, take each French scene and break it into pantomime phrases. Then put in vital dialogue.

ly two lines of dialogue. However, many groups would not play the scene this way. Instead, they might use a running commentary similar to the following:

CINDERELLA: How lonesome it is sitting here in the garden while everyone has gone to the ball. A flash of light. What can it be?!
FAIRY GODMOTHER: I am your Fairy Godmother, Cinderella. Just watch me. Do you see this stalk? I will wave my magic wand and I will change this stalk into a beautiful red flower. Watch! I am waving my wand.
CINDERELLA: Oh, you have changed that stalk into a beautiful red flower! I cannot believe my eyes. How wonderful! You must be a real Fairy Godmother!
FAIRY GODMOTHER: Yes I am your Fairy Godmother, Cinderella.

Personality and Character Development. Before you can begin rehearsing the script, you must analyze each character's age, sex, occupation, and ethnic background. The more the director understands each role, the better he or she can guide the cast in bringing their characters to life.

Group discussion of the characters is also important. Who are the characters? What is their background? How would they react in a specific situation? How would they move? How would their voices sound? The entire group should participate in the process of character development.

The characters must always be consistent. For example, if Cinderella were on the moon she would still be Cinderella. She would still be beautiful, hard working, generous, and kind.

The best way to get to know the character is to improvise with it. Start with pantomime. Suppose Cinderella were given a box. How would she try to open it? Would her movements differ from those of her sisters if they were given a box? Imagine Cinderella in the garden crying. How would she react if a frog jumped up and sat in her lap? How would her sisters react?

You should encourage the members of the group to be as original as possible in their im-provisations. It is through im-provisation that new material is brought to the group. Young people may tend to imitate television; this should be discouraged. Each child should be encouraged to develop his or her own puppet character.

Make sure that there are no characters with similar voices or patterns of movement. Similar voices are especially distracting as the audience may not know which puppet is speaking.

Avoid stereotypes. The girl is not always sweet and helpless; the boy is not always strong and active. Also avoid religious, racial, and cultural stereotypes.

Padding. Padding refers to adding anything unnecessary to a script to make it longer. This is as common as it is undesirable. It is better to have two short plays than one long, needlessly drawn out play.

If there are any questions about whether a show is padded or not, ask, "Is the additional material necessary?" If it is not justified, it would be better to leave it out.

Chapter

5

Design

In the theatre world, a production will have designated designers for sets, costumes, and lighting. The theatre director has knowledge of these areas and complete control over them. This principle applies equally to the director of puppet theatre.

Three elements are involved in the design of a puppet production: style, period, and color. The director must use these elements to design sets, scenery, puppets, costumes, props (hand props and stage props), and light and sound so that all harmonize to create a unified production.

Style. Legitimate theatre recognizes eight major style forms: naturalism, realism, impressionism, expressionism, formalism, constructivism, symbolism, and stylization. Most puppet productions use two of these styles: realism and stylization.

In selecting a style, you must relate it to the type of play being presented and the type of puppets being used. Once the style is chosen, it dictates the entire production.

Period. Any historical period may be chosen for the setting of a play—contemporary, medieval, ancient, the roaring 20s, and so on. Whatever peri-

Stage design showing a realistic setting. Design by Carol Fijan.

36

Stage design showing a *stylization* setting. Design by Carol Fijan.

od is selected, it must fit the author's general concept.

If the play is a folk tale set in another country, the group might investigate the dress of the people in that country. Native costumes have remained virtually unchanged over the years.

Color. A production will have either a loose or a tight color combination. A loose combination uses many colors; a tight combination uses values of two or three colors. For example, the entire production could be in blue and lavender. Black and white are not considered colors and can be used in either type of combination. Both loose and tight combinations have their advantages and disadvantages.

A positive aspect of a loose combination is that many colors can be used. This is especially desirable in a school situation. If children are making their own puppets, they can make them the colors that they like best. The negative aspect of a loose combination is that the production may end up with so many colors that nothing stands out or has any real dramatic impact.

TRADE SECRET

If the production is presented in a school, researching an historical period could be a good class exercise.

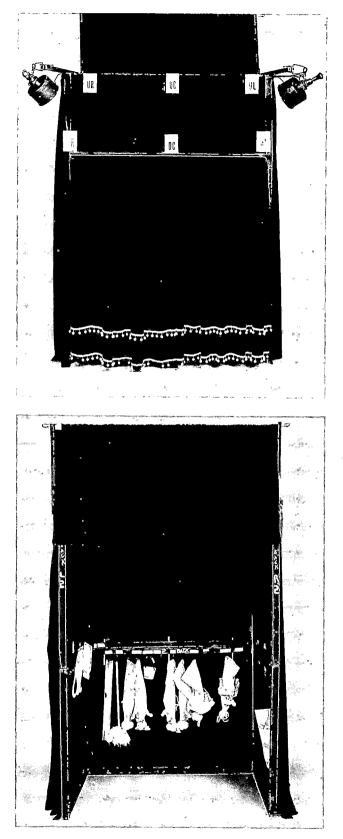

A tight combination, on the other hand, contributes to a unified play. It can, however, become monotonous.

Whether loose or tight, there are certain rules regarding color. The color must suit the mood of the play and the mood of the characters. Color must be used to distinguish characters from each other when they appear in the same scene. Be very careful not to blend the color of a puppet and the background.

Whatever your preference, you must be consistent in the use of color in all aspects of the design. This is the only real rule of color coordination.

Set Design. Set design is the environment of the play. It can range from the bare stage to elaborate scenery.

In designing sets, it is essential that you be aware of sight lines so that the audience can see all the action and scenery.

The placing of entrances and exits is important. In our culture we read from left to right. Place entrances and exits in the most effective spots to highlight some and downplay others.

TOP: Front view of standing stage: 4' wide x 6' high x 3' deep.

BOTTOM: Back view of standing stage.

Stages. The design of a stage is dictated by the type of puppets used and by the height of the puppeteers. The stage should be constructed so that is can be packed into a car or other means of transportation.

TOP: Front view of five-panel folding floor screen: 5' high.

BOTTOM: Back view of five-panel folding floor screen.

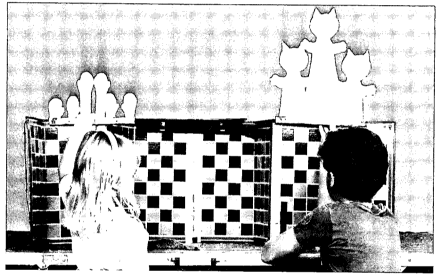

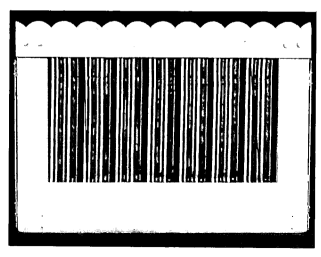

TOP: Front view of checkerboard folding-table stage.

MIDDLE: Back view of checkerboard folding-table stage.

BOTTOM: Front view of table stage: approximately 4' wide x 33" high x 14" deep.

TOP: Back view of table stage.

MIDDLE: Front view of wooden table screen: four panels 2' high x 20'' wide.

BOTTOM: Back view of wooden table screen.

Puppets. Puppets must be made in the style and the period chosen. Consider whether the puppeteers are adults who can handle bigger and heavier puppets or children able to manipulate lighter, hand puppets.

Puppets should be not only beautiful but, more important, easily manipulated.

Costumes. Costumes should be simple and visible from the back of the auditorium. If the costume is from a specific period, the design of the period should be emphasized. If, for example, the dress has a bouffant skirt, emphasize that line and simplify the rest.

When looking for materials that carry, be certain that any pattern in the material can be seen from a distance.

Today we have such knitted materials as nylon or orlon acrylic, which drape well and pack without creasing. This should be taken into consideration when designing a costume and choosing the fabric for it.

TOP: Examples of good and bad costume design. Puppet on left is dressed simply. Puppet on right is overdressed; such design will not carry at a distance. Design by Carol Fijan.
MIDDLE: Bad floral fabric design will not carry at a distance. Design by Kathy Kane.
BOTTOM: Example of good fabric design. Mother Earth, from *The Enchanted Forest*, Teen Concert Theatre (Great Neck, NY). Design by Carol Fijan.

TRADE SECRET

To effect a costume change, do not change the costume on the puppet. Change to an identical puppet with a different costume.

Use of large bucket as stage prop. *Holiday for Mice*, National Puppet Productions. Design by Paul Vincent-Davis.

Props. Props are objects used by a puppet. There are two kinds: hand props and stage props. Hand props refer to items used by a puppet, such as a fan, cup, mop, or handkerchief. Stage props are parts of the scenery, such as a chair, a magic mirror, or a spinning wheel.

Do not clutter the stage with unnecessary props. The only justification for a prop is its necessity for plot development.

Example of a hand prop. *Holiday for Mice*, National Puppet Productions. Design by Paul-Vincent Davis; costume by Carol Fijan.

TRADE SECRET

It is good to go shopping for fabrics with someone. Have that person hold the material up and go to the other end of the store to see if the color and pattern come across or if it is just a muddle. Textured materials may look fuzzy up close, but smooth from far away.

The "real" puppet (Cat) and the work puppet (cat). *The Sorcerer's Den,* Teen Concert Theatre (Great Neck, NY). Design by Paul Vincent-Davis.

Example of a work prop (stick). *Kismet,* University of Connecticut, directed by Frank Ballard. Design by Frank Ballard.

Work Puppets and Work Props. Since rehearsing the play and building the puppets and props occur simultaneously, work props and puppets are necessary for daily rehearsals. They should be made quickly by the group and should be as much as possible like the ones to be used in the performance.

Making work puppets and work props is as essential a part of the schedule as is making the final puppets and props. To lessen wear and tear, do not use the finished puppets and props until the final rehearsals.

Lighting. The function of lighting for any theatrical production is twofold: it illuminates the scene, and it

Do not make the finished puppets first and then go into rehearsal because the puppet character may be eliminated from the final script.

The real prop (spear).

helps establish mood through the use of color and intensity. The audience should have no problem seeing what is happening on stage. Even if the lights are dimmed to create a dark, mysterious mood or cave-like setting, there must still be sufficient illumination for them to see the action.

Most puppet plays require simple lighting. Usually, two lights are sufficient and these should be mounted in front of the proscenium arch. Front cross-lighting positions allow the face of the puppet to be visible when the puppet is downstage (Diagram 4). Lights placed directly overhead will cast a shadow on the face of the puppet.

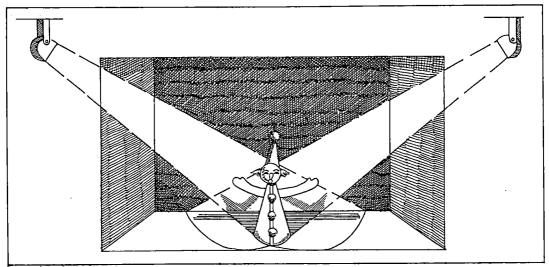

Diagram 4: Front cross-lighting

Example of a work hand puppet and work stage prop. Design in a class exercise.

Example of the finished puppet and the stage prop. *"Where Are You, Cinderella?"* Kathy Kane Puppets. Design by Kathy Kane.

These gels come in a wide variety of hues; usually a light pink or a pale straw will work well for the average puppet production. You can purchase them from theatrical lighting firms.

Sound. Sound in a production is divided into music, sound effects, and voice.

Music. Music in a puppet play is effective as an interlude between scenes and when the scenery is being changed. It can be used as theme music to identify characters. It can build or change moods. Of course, it can also be used for overtures

You may wish to highlight a certain character or prop. To accomplish this, a specially placed light focused on the subject should be used (Diagram 5).

Avoid the use of straight "white" light. It is best to soften the lighting by using either colored bulbs or by placing a theatrical color medium over the light source. The color medium is referred to as a gelatin ("gel") or by a brand name such as Roscolene.

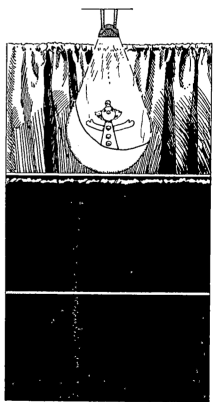

Diagram 5: Front head-on lighting

46

Although a "gel" resembles colored plastic or cellophane, take care not to substitute those materials for the real gelatin. Cellophane and plastic are not made to withstand the tremendous heat that is generated by the bulbs and may melt or catch fire.

and for dances and musical numbers in the show.

Music can be recorded or live. Most puppet groups use recorded music. Sometimes they are fortunate enough to have original music written for their production. In any event, be aware of copyright laws, or try to use music in the public domain.

Sound Effects. There are hundreds of sound effects, including everything from water dripping to the collapse of a huge building. Recordings of these sound effects are readily available. Use sound effects only when needed; for example, in *"Where Are You, Cinderella"* the clock striking twelve is an important and necessary sound effect.

Voice. A good puppet voice should be scaled to the size of the puppet. It should reflect the character and personality of the puppet. It is the director's responsibility to see that the puppeteer does not sacrifice clarity of diction and audibility when developing a puppet voice.

Live voice productions have the virtue of spontaneity. Any backstage emergency can be covered; for instance, when a prop falls or a puppet breaks, the puppeteer can improvise. He or she can also deal with a heckler in the audience or encourage audience participation.

For a small fee, most lighting companies will send a booklet of gelatin color samples. Try each sample in front of the lights to see what effect that hue will have on the puppets and scenery.

Because tapes can break, keep a second tape and a backup tape recorder on hand. When a tape breaks, the puppeteer will have to stop the show and change the broken tape if two recorders are not playing at the same time. Always buy the best quality tape and cassettes to minimize breakage and to enhance the sound.

Many puppeteers tape the sound of their entire production, including the voices. A voice can be either that of a puppeteer who creates and manipulates the character or that of a professional actor. If professional actors' voices are used, the actors should work closely with the puppeteers who are playing the parts before the voices are recorded. In all cases, the puppets' actions must be synchronized with the taped voices. This means rehearsal.

One of the positive aspects of using taped voices is that any puppeteer can manipulate a male or female puppet once the actor's voice is on tape. In addition, a puppeteer in a complicated show can concentrate on manipulating the puppet, *not* on projecting his or her voice, working too close to a microphone, or wearing a mike and getting entangled in the wires.

There are several negative aspects of using taped voices. If there is a "flub" in the action, what does the puppeteer do? If the audience laughs in an unexpected place, what does the puppeteer do? The tape cannot be stopped for the puppeteer to react.

Often puppeteers do not feel the same attachment to a puppet if they are manipulating it

If using taped voices or music, a work tape for rehearsals and a good copy for performances is necessary.

to someone else's voice. If taped voices are used, the puppeteers should mouth the words as they manipulate the characters so they feel more involved. But even with this additional interaction, a taped show tends to become stale.

If the show is live, it is a good idea to make one taping of a performance for the record.

Chapter

6

Casting

Whether a group is large or small, amateur or professional, when casting a play everyone should have an equal chance. However, as in all phases of a production, you make the final decision.

Let the whole group know beforehand what roles will be cast as well as the time and place of auditions. Try to make the time as convenient as possible for the majority of the group.

You might have T-shirts made for the technical crew with "tech crew" printed on them.

The qualifications you are looking for should be made known to those trying out for the parts. Puppeteers should be tested for imagination and their ability to think on their feet. Improvisation will also give you information on how many different puppet voices each person can do with ease.

Test how well the puppeteer manipulates the puppet. The types of puppets to be used in the production should be available to those auditioning. If the production is a live musical, the puppeteer's singing ability must be tested. If the musical is recorded, you should have several records of songs on hand to see how well the puppeteer can synchronize to the soundtrack.

After casting is complete, how should you deal with casting disappointments? You must make yourself available to every member of the group to explain the choices for the various roles. Each person must have the chance to ask you why he or she did not get a certain role, and you should answer questions as fully as possible. In this way you can show that there was no favoritism in awarding the part. Those who did not get a lead may be understudies or play other roles. Let the group know that auditions are a learning experience. Periodic assessment of one's strengths and weaknesses are essential to continued growth as a puppeteer.

You should hold auditions for the technical staff as well. This includes those who will work on lights, sound, scenery, damaged puppets, props, and any miscellaneous backstage work needed during a production. Everyone must be made aware that working on the technical crew is as vital as manipulating the puppets. Without a good tech crew, you might not have a good production. Be sure to thank each member of the tech crew individually (Diagrams 6 & 7).

AUDITION FORM

Last name_____   First name_____

Home address_____Telephone #_____

_____

Height_____   (Age_____)

Previous experience:

    Acting_____

    _____

    Puppetry_____

    _____

    Singing_____

    _____

    Dance_____

    _____

Tryout preference: Speaking role_____   Non-speaking role_____

(see reverse side)

Diagram 6: Front side of an audition form

List the times you CANNOT rehearse:

Mon._____   Fri._____

Tues._____   Sat._____

Wed._____   Sun._____

Thurs._____

<u>   DO NOT WRITE BELOW THIS LINE   </u>

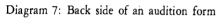

	1	2	3	4	5	REMARKS
IM	☐	☐	☐	☐	☐	
VO	☐	☐	☐	☐	☐	
SI	☐	☐	☐	☐	☐	
MA	☐	☐	☐	☐	☐	

SCALE: 1=low   5=high   DATE:____/____/____/

IM = improvisation
VO = voice characterization
SI = singing
MA = manipulation

Diagram 7: Back side of an audition form

Chapter

The Production Book

An indispensable tool for you is the production or prompt book. This is the master script of the production. It contains all the notations regarding blocking and technical effects. It should contain lists of costume changes, props, set changes, a rehearsal schedule, and other similar necessary items.

Although you should have the major portion of the blocking clearly stated in the prompt book before the rehearsals

All notations in the prompt book should be recorded in pencil so that changes can be made easily. Use different-colored pencils for light and sound cues.

start, you are not infallible. Events may occur during rehearsals that will necessitate changes in your original ideas.

Each movement the puppet makes, each light and sound cue, must be marked where you wish it to occur at the specific word or action in the script.

If you are working with a musical piece, the music score becomes the prompt book.

A loose-leaf binder makes an ideal holder for the production book. It allows pages to be added or deleted.

Blocking can be conveniently recorded in the binder in the following way: Include in the binder a blank piece of paper for each page of the script. Each item of blocking is marked by a number placed in a circle at the point where it is to occur in the script. These numbers can then be recorded on the blank page along with the description of what happens and/or a diagram of the movement to which they refer.

BLOCKING TERMINOLOGY

Stage directions are always given from the puppet's point of view as it faces the audience.

In conjunction with the initials of the acting areas, the following symbols are used to record blocking:

At rise: at the rise of the curtain (the beginning of a scene)
X: cross
Xing: crossing; go toward, in the direction of
R: right
L: left
C: center
UR: upper right
UL: upper left
UC: upper center
DR: down right
DL: down left
DC: down center

In addition to these symbols, the following are used for light and sound cues:

LITES or LT: lights
S or SD: sound

Light and sound cues are recorded on the righthand side of the script They too are numbered. These numbers are placed inside a square, (e.g.,

Save your production book for use in future class work.

$\boxed{\text{LT 1}}$ or $\boxed{\text{SD 1}}$) to distinguish them from the action numerals, which are placed inside circles (e.g., ①   ).

Puppet characters are identified either by the abbreviation of their names or by placing their initials in a triangle.

In the production *"Where Are You, Cinderella,?"* we use the following abbreviations for the puppets:

HFGM: Head Fairy Godmother
CAS: Cassandra
GR: Gretchen
BR: Brunhilda
CIN: Cinderella

The following script is our version of the fairy tale *Cinderella*. It is presented with the complete blocking of the puppets' actions, together with lists of the characters, scenery, special effects, and props, both hand and stage. This play can be presented on a simple puppet stage.

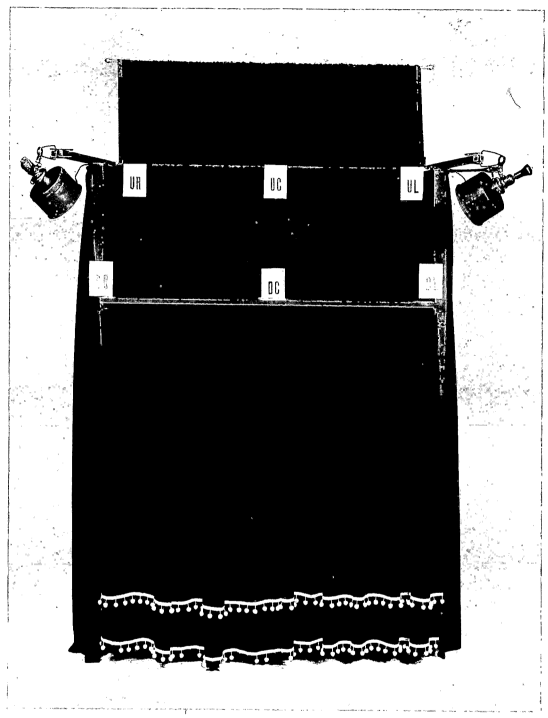

Front of stage indicating stage positions. *"Where Are You, Cinderella?"* Kathy Kane Puppets. Design by Kathy Kane.

"WHERE ARE YOU, CINDERELLA?"

Production Notes
    Puppets
    Scenery
    Stage Props
    Hand Props
    Special Effects
Complete Blocking

"WHERE ARE YOU, CINDERELLA?"

PRODUCTION NOTES

Puppets (in order of appearance):
  1. Four clusters of Stars
  2. Head Fairy Godmother
  3. Cassandra, the Fairy Godmother who must earn her wings
  4. A royal Page on horseback
  5. Gretchen, a tall, angular sister
  6. Brunhilda, a short, fat sister
  7. Cinderella (in work clothes)
  8. A little Bird
  9. Cinderella (in ball gown)
10. Four dancing Couples
11. Prince Charming
12. Prince Charming on horseback
13. A royal Page on foot

Scenery (on lower level unless otherwise stated):

Item	Scene	Location
Large scroll	Prologue	UL
Dressing screen (with initial "G")	Act I, Scene 2	R
Dressing screen (with initial "B")	Act I, Scene 2	L

(The screens can be made of either curtains or cardboard.)

Vines and pumpkins		
(coach effect is part of this)	Act I, Scene 3	R
Corn stalks	Act I, Scene 3	L
Royal Hanging	Act II, Scene 2	R
Royal Hanging	Act II, Scene 2	L

Stage Props:

Item	Scene
Rectangular bathtub	Act I, Scene 2
Round bathtub	Act I, Scene 2
Rectangular jewelry box	Act I, Scene 2
Round jewelry box	Act I, Scene 2

Hand Props:

Item	Scene	Used by
Wand	All scenes	Cassandra
Trumpet	Act I, Scene 1; Act II, Scene 2	Page on horseback
String of beads	Act I, Scene 2	Gretchen
Fans, shoes, gloves	Act I, Scene 2	Cinderella
Broom	Act I, Scene 2	Cassandra
Basket of laundry	Act I, Scene 3	Cinderella
Slipper	Act II, Scene 1	Prince
Pillow with slipper	Act II, Scene 3	Page on foot
Wings	Act II, Scene 3	Cassandra
End sign	Act II, Scene 3	Bird

Special Effects:

Item	Scene	Used by
Puff of smoke	Prologue	Head Fairy Godmother
Stalk into flower	Act I, Scene 3	Cassandra
Pumpkin into coach	Act I, Scene 3; Act II, Scene 3	Cassandra
Fairy Wand	Optional	
Fairy wings appear	Act II, Scene 3	Cassandra

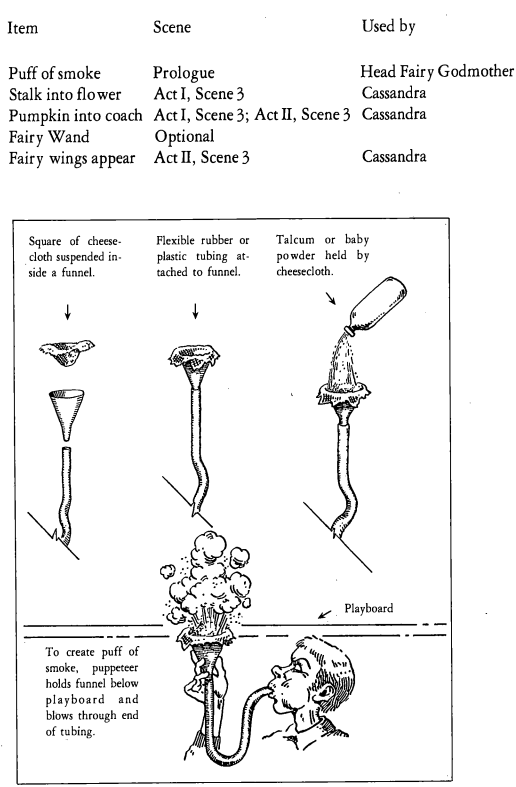

Square of cheese-cloth suspended inside a funnel.

Flexible rubber or plastic tubing attached to funnel.

Talcum or baby powder held by cheesecloth.

Playboard

To create puff of smoke, puppeteer holds funnel below playboard and blows through end of tubing.

Diagram 8a: Puff of smoke

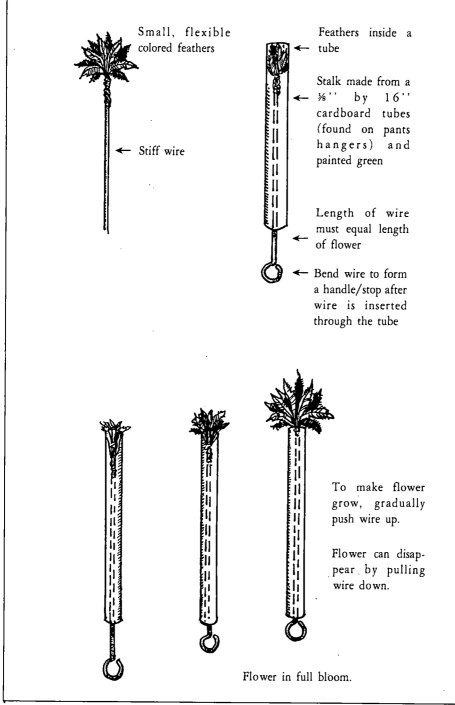

Small, flexible colored feathers

Feathers inside a tube

Stalk made from a ⅜'' by 16'' cardboard tubes (found on pants hangers) and painted green

← Stiff wire

Length of wire must equal length of flower

Bend wire to form a handle/stop after wire is inserted through the tube

To make flower grow, gradually push wire up.

Flower can disappear by pulling wire down.

Flower in full bloom.

Diagram 8b: Stalk into flower

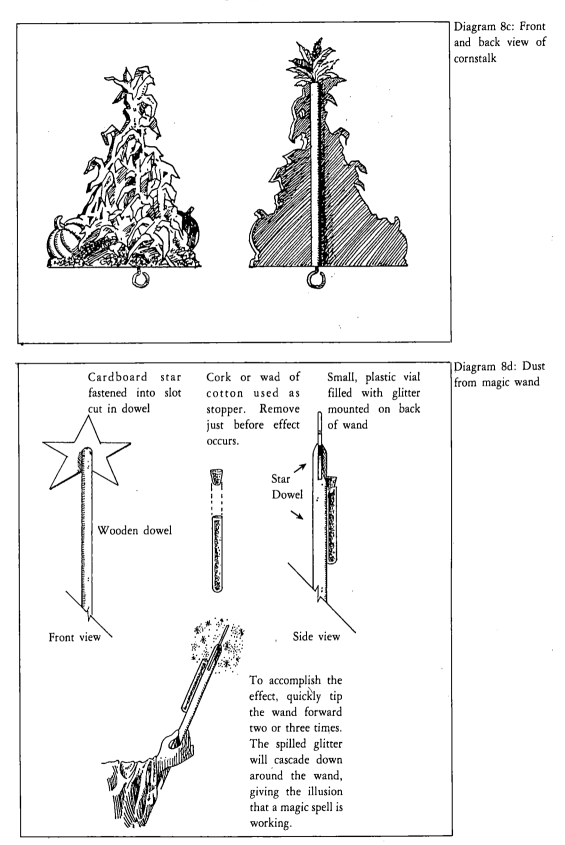

Diagram 8c: Front and back view of cornstalk

Diagram 8d: Dust from magic wand

Cardboard star fastened into slot cut in dowel

Cork or wad of cotton used as stopper. Remove just before effect occurs.

Small, plastic vial filled with glitter mounted on back of wand

Wooden dowel

Star
Dowel

Front view

Side view

To accomplish the effect, quickly tip the wand forward two or three times. The spilled glitter will cascade down around the wand, giving the illusion that a magic spell is working.

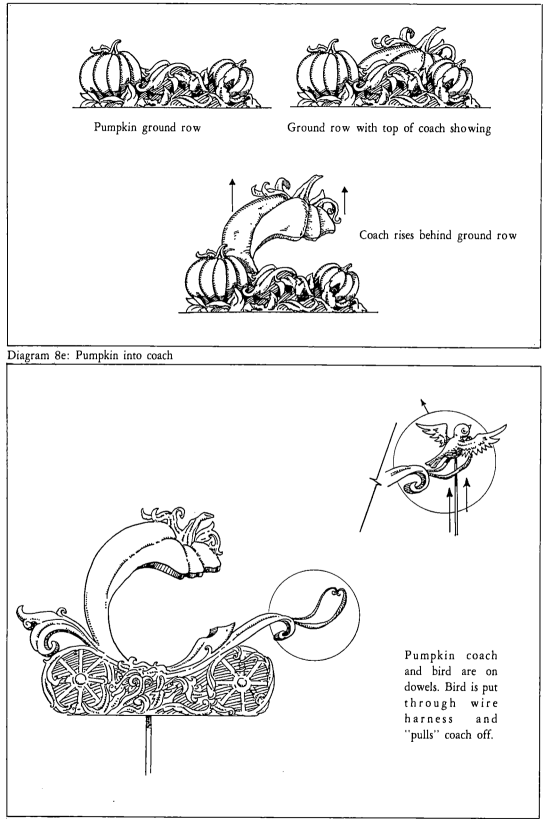

Pumpkin ground row

Ground row with top of coach showing

Coach rises behind ground row

Diagram 8e: Pumpkin into coach

Pumpkin coach and bird are on dowels. Bird is put through wire harness and "pulls" coach off.

Diagram 8f: Bird into harness

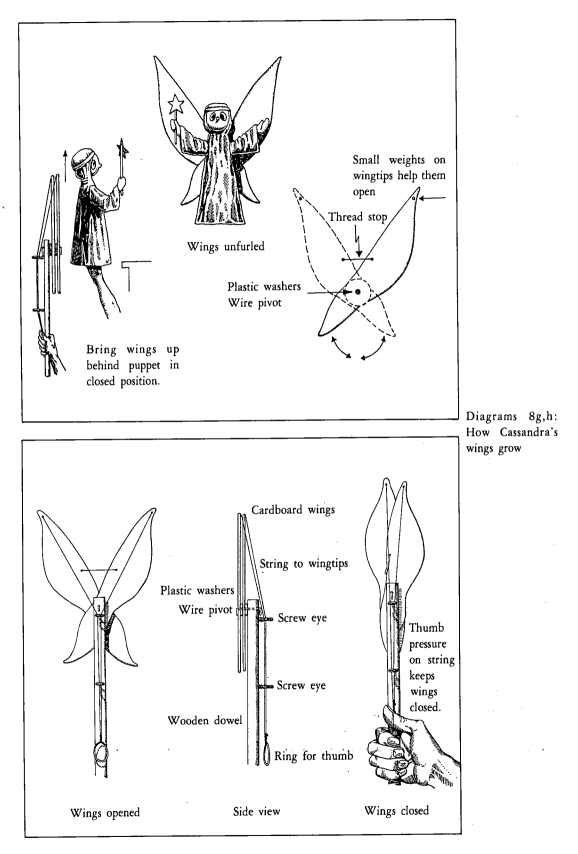

Wings unfurled

Small weights on wingtips help them open

Thread stop

Plastic washers
Wire pivot

Bring wings up behind puppet in closed position.

Diagrams 8g,h: How Cassandra's wings grow

Cardboard wings

String to wingtips

Plastic washers
Wire pivot

Screw eye

Screw eye

Wooden dowel

Ring for thumb

Thumb pressure on string keeps wings closed.

Wings opened

Side view

Wings closed

"WHERE ARE YOU, CINDERELLA?"

PROLOGUE

SETTING: *Somewhere in space. At rise, the stage is dimly lit, but there is enough light for one to see that the playing area is divided into two levels. Stars of varying size and color float around on both levels. As the lights slowly come up, the HEAD FAIRY GOD-MOTHER is discovered on the upper level,* ① *looking at a long scroll.*

MUSIC: *up, under, and out*

HEAD FAIRY GODMOTHER: *(calling)* ② Cassandra...Cassandra, ③ where ④ are you?

CASSANDRA: *(appearing on lower level)* ⑤ Here I am, Head Fairy Godmother!

HEAD FAIRY GODMOTHER: I have been looking over the master ⑥ list and I see that ⑦ you have not earned your fairy ⑧ wings. Why not?

Note: four clusters of Stars: A, B, C, D

1. At rise:
   HFGM → UL at scroll
   Star business: A enters DR; exits DL
      B enters UL; exits UR
      C enters DL; exits DR
      D enters UR; exits UL

   Note: stars raise, lower, and spin around as they X stage; movement should vary.

2. Xing → UR
3. Xing → UL
4. Xing → UC

5. pops up from below, DR

6. turns UL; points to list
7. points → CAS
8. Xs quickly R; bends over looking down at CAS

Prologue: Head Fairy Godmother and Cassandra, who must earn her fairy wings. *"Where Are You, Cinderella?"* Kathy Kane Puppets. Design by Kathy Kane.

CASSANDRA: I try very had to work our ⑨
magic spells. But something always goes ⑩
wrong.

HEAD FAIRY GODMOTHER: (*thinking*)
Well, I will give you one more chance. ⑪

CASSANDRA: Thank you, thank you! I will ⑫ ⑬
try very hard to get everything right.

HEAD FAIRY GODMOTHER: (*consulting
the list*) Pick a letter from "A" to "Z!" ⑭

CASSANDRA: (*thinking*) "C!" I pick the ⑮ ⑯
letter "C."

HEAD FAIRY GODMOTHER: (*looking
at the list*) "C"...here it is. "C" stands for ⑰ ⑱
"Cinderella." You are to see that Cinderella
goes to a ball, dances with a prince, and then
marries him!

CASSANDRA: Highest of all Fairy ⑲
Godmothers, how am I to do all that?

HEAD FAIRY GODMOTHER: That is up ⑳
to you, Cassandra. But, if Cinderella does not ㉑
marry a prince, you will never receive your ㉒
fairy wings. I have spoken! (*Exits.*) ㉓ ㉔

CASSANDRA: (*sighs*) Oh, dear! (*Looks ㉕ ㉖
around.*) Where are you, Cinderella? (*Exits as ㉗
the lights dim to blackout.*)

9. trembles, turns R, shaking her head
10. turns → HFGM

11. scratches her head with right hand \9
12. bows to HFGM
13. bows to HFGM

14. Xs → list, UL
15. turns front, holding her head
16. turns quickly → HFGM

17. looking for the right place in the list, then quickly pointing to it when she finds it
18. turns → CAS

19. bows to HFGM

20. turns → list
21. turns quickly → CAS
22. points menacingly → CAS
23. turns front
24. exits in puff of smoke
25. holding her head; moving it from side to side
26. looks around
27. Xs quickly DL, exits

Act I, Scene 1: Page on Horse, announcing the Ball.

ACT I, Scene 1

SETTING: *The top level represents a street. At rise, the stage is bare.*

MUSIC: *trumpet fanfare*

A PAGE on horseback enters. He holds a trumpet in his downstage hand.

PAGE: Hear ye! Hear ye! Prince Charming is ① giving a ball. All the ladies of the land are in- ② vited. At this ball, he will choose one young lady to be his bride. Hear ③ ye! Hear ④ ye! All the ladies of the land are invited. (*Exits; lights dim on top level.*)

1. enters UR; speaks as Xs → UC
2. stops; turns DC
3. turns UL
4. speaks as he exits UL

Act I, Scene 2: The two Sisters fight to possess the beads before going to the Ball.

ACT I, Scene 2

SETTING: *A room in Cinderella's house. On each side of the stage is a dressing screen. The one on the right bears the initial "G," while the screen on the left displays the initial "B."*

As the scene opens, GRETCHEN is alone on stage admiring a long string of beads.

GRETCHEN: ① If I wear these beads to the ball, the Prince will surely choose me to be his bride.

1. holding up beads

BRUNHILDA: *(entering)* ② You can't wear those beads!

2. enters L

GRETCHEN: ③ Why not?

3. turns → BR

BRUNHILDA: ④ Because they're mine!

4. Xs R; grabs beads

GRETCHEN: ⑤ No! They're *mine!*

5. pulls beads away from BR

(The two sisters tug at the string of beads, screaming at each other: "They're ⑥ mine!"

6. BR grabs heads again; tug-of-war business

"No, they're mine!" "Mine!" At last, each gives a violent tug at the beads and the string breaks, spilling the beads all over the floor.)

GRETCHEN: *(looking down at the floor)* ⑦ Just look what you've done! Now no one can wear them to the ⑧ ball!

7. looking down

8. exits R behind screen

BRUNHILDA: Cinderella can pick them up. ⑨ We had better get dressed. *(Exits behind her screen.)*

9. exits L behind screen

GRETCHEN: Where are you, Cinderella? ⑩

Bring me my bath! (*Exits behind her screen.* ⑪

CINDERELLA *enters, pushing a large, rectangular bathtub, which she places behind GRETCHEN'S screen.*) ⑫

BRUNHILDA: (*from behind screen*) Where are you, Cinderella? Bring me my bath! ⑬ (*CINDERELLA pulls onstage a large, round bathtub filled with bubbles and places it behind BRUNHILDA'S screen.*) Now bring me my jewels, Cinderella! (*CINDERELLA* ⑭ *pulls onstage a round jewelry box and puts it behind the left screen.*)

GRETCHEN: (*from behind the screen*) Bring me my jewels, Cinderella! (*CINDER-* ⑮ *ELLA pushes onstage a square jewelry box and puts it behind the right screen.*)

BRUNHILDA: Cinderella, help me with my ⑯ dress!

GRETCHEN: Cinderella, help me with my ⑰ dress!

(*The two sisters keep calling for CINDER-ELLA, demanding that she bring them such things as shoes, gloves, fans, etc.*) *CIN-DERELLA runs frantically between the screens until she finally collapses from* ⑱ *exhaustion.*

The sisters emerge from behind their ⑲ *respective screens dressed in their ball gowns.*)

BRUNHILDA: Don't I look beautiful? ⑳

10.	pokes out her head
11.	head disappears behind screen
12.	enters R, pushing tub; puts it behind R screen
13.	CIN exits L; returns pulling tub; puts it behind L screen
14.	CIN exits L; returns pulling jewel box; puts it behind L screen
15.	CIN exits R; returns pushing jewel box; puts it behind R screen
16.	CIN runs behind L screen
17.	CIN runs behind R screen
18.	CIN runs between screens and exits bringing props; CIN collapses DC
19.	Sisters enter from behind screens dressed in ball gowns
20.	Xing L

GRETCHEN: (21) Don't I look even more beautiful?

21. Xing R

(22) (*They turn to leave.*)

22. Xs L

GRETCHEN: (23) (*sweetly*) Cinderella, you may go to the ball, too.

BRUNHILDA: (23) (*sweetly*)Yes, Cinderella. All the young ladies of the land are invited.

23. turning → CIN

CINDERELLA: (24) Oh, thank you sisters!

24. bowing

GRETCHEN: (25) (*cruelly*) You may go as soon as you sweep the floor, make the beds, do the dishes, wash the windows, iron the clothes...

25. turning → L

BRUNHILDA: (26) (*cruelly*) ...and cook us a great big dinner!

26. turning → L

(27) (*The two sisters exeunt, laughing at their joke.*)

27. exeunt L

CINDERELLA: (28) (*starts to cry*) I'll never get to the ball if I have to do all that! (29) (*Picks up a broom as the lights fade.*)

28. hands to face, crying

29. exits R

Act I, Scene 3: Cinderella meets Cassandra, her Fairy Godmother, in the garden.

ACT I, Scene 3

SETTING: *The garden outside Cinderella's home. On the left is a large cornstalk. On the right, among a tangle of vines, can be seen the top of a large pumpkin. A BIRD is sitting on the cornstalk.*

As the lights come up, CINDERELLA ① *enters carrying a basket of laundry. She puts* ② *it down and, with a long, sad sigh, sits down* ③ *on the pumpkin.*

1. CIN enters R
2. basket DR; sighs
3. sits L side of pumpkin

The little BIRD, feeling sorry for her, flies ④ *down from the cornstalk and perches on a vine nearby. CINDERELLA reaches out to pet the* ⑤ *BIRD. It hops back, frightened. She extends* ⑥ ⑦ *her hand and holds it still. The BIRD moves* ⑧ *closer. It carefully looks at her hand, decides* ⑨ *she means no harm, and with a happy chirp,* ⑩ *hops onto her finger. CINDERELLA laughs* ⑪ *happily.*

4. sits LC of CIN

5. CIN reaches for BIRD
6. BIRD → CIN
7. CIN holds out hand → BIRD
8. BIRD hops → R
9. BIRD looks

10. BIRD hops onto her hand; chirps
11. CIN laughs

Suddenly, there is a flash of light. CIN- ⑫ ⑬ *DERELLA jumps up, startled, and the BIRD* ⑭ *flies quickly onto the cornstalk. CASSAN-* ⑮ *DRA appears.*

12. light flash
13. CIN jumps up
14. BIRD flies → stalk

15. CAS pops up

CINDERELLA: Who are you? Where did ⑯ ⑰ you come from?

16. step → CAS
17. step → CAS

CASSANDRA: I am your fairy godmother, Cinderella.

CINDERELLA: You can't be my fairy god- ⑱ mother. You don't have wings!

18. looks behind CAS's back

72

CASSANDRA: I know, I know. But I *can* do

magic, sometimes. Watch! (*She waves her* | 19. waves wand; stalk into flower
wand and transforms a cornstalk into a flower.
Amazed at her own powers,) It worked. It
really worked!

CINDERELLA: (*overjoyed*) Oh, you really

can do magic! (*She runs to CASSANDRA* | 20. Xs → CAS; kneels
and kneels before her.)

CASSANDRA: Get up, Cinderella. We must | 21. helps CIN up
dress you for the ball.

CINDERELLA: But I have nothing to wear.

CASSANDRA: I'll take care of that! (*She* | 22. pushes CIN behind stalk
pushes CINDERELLA behind the cornstalk,
raises her wand, and chants,) | 23. waves wand
   Abra-ca-dabra, feather and fess.
   Magic and moonlight,
   Make me a dress!

(*To herself,*) I hope I got the right spell.
(*Calls to CINDERELLA,*) Come out now, | 24. turns → stalk
Cinderella. Let me see how you look. (*CIN-*
DERELLA comes out still in her old dress.) | 25. CIN enters from behind stalk
Oh, no! What did I do wrong? Go back and | 26. hands to head
I'll try again. | 27. tries to push CIN behind stalk

CINDERELLA: Even if you can make me a | 28. shaking head "no"
dress, how am I going to get to the ball?

CASSANDRA: I can handle that! (*She waves* | 29. turns → pumpkin; waves
| wand
her wand and the pumpkin rises out of the | 30. coach appears
vines as an open coach.) It worked! It | 31. jumping up and down

73

㉜ worked! There, Cinderella, you have a coach to take you to the ball.	32. turns → CIN
CINDERELLA: But I still have nothing to wear.	
CASSANDRA: ㉝ (*pushing her back behind the cornstalk again*) I'll get it right this time! (*Chants,*) Abra-ca-dabra, feather and fess. Magic and moonlight, Make me a dress!	33. pushes CIN behind stalk
CINDERELLA: (*returning in the same dress*) ㉞ It's alright, Fairy Godmother. I don't have to go to the ball.	34. entering from behind stalk
CASSANDRA: Oh, yes you do. You have to go to the ball or else I will never earn my fairy wings. Go ㉟ back and I'll try once more! (*CINDERELLA goes slowly and reluctantly behind the cornstalk again.*)	35. pushes CIN behind stalk
CASSANDRA: What am I doing ㊱ wrong? (*Thinks.*) I know! I forgot to tap three times after I wave my magic wand.	36. hands to head
㊲ Abra-ca-dabra, feather and ㊳ fess. Magic and ㊴ moonlight, Make me a ㊵ dress!	37. waves wand 38. taps once 39. taps once 40. taps once
(*CINDERELLA* ㊶ *comes out in her ball gown.*) It ㊷ worked! It worked!	41. CIN enters in ball gown 42. jumping up and down
CINDERELLA: ㊸ Thank you, Fairy Godmother. It's beautiful!	43. bows

CASSANDRA: No time for thanks now. You'll be late for the ball. Quickly now, into ④④ the coach! (*She helps CINDERELLA into the coach. Then she motions to the BIRD, ④⑤ who comes down and gets into the harness.* Remember, Cinderella, you must be home before the clock strikes midnight!

44. helps CIN into coach

45. turns → BIRD; it flies into harness

CINDERELLA: I'll remember. (*Coach starts ④⑥ off.*) But Fairy Godmother, who is going to ④⑦ do my housework?

46. nods "yes"; coach starts → L

47. turns back → CAS

CASSANDRA: I will, Cinderella. Have a good ④⑧ time!

48. waves

(*The BIRD flies off, pulling the coach behind ④⑨ it. CASSANDRA picks up the laundry ⑤⓪ basket.*)

49. coach exits L

50. picks up basket

CASSANDRA: I wish there were a magic spell to do housework! (*The lights fade out.*) ⑤①

51. exits R

Act II, Scene 1: In the castle ballroom, the Prince faints when he meets the beautiful Cinderella.

ACT II, Scene 1

SETTING: *The Ballroom in the castle. On either side of the stage are royal hangings. Music is heard and, as the scene opens, dancing couples are moving across both levels of the stage.* ①

   The PRINCE enters, ② *dancing with GRETCHEN. She* ③ *steps on his toes. He* ④ *groans and limps out with her. More dancers cross* ⑤ *the stage.*

   The PRINCE enters, ⑥ *dancing with BRUNHILDA. They do a* ⑦ *dip. He drops her and she* ⑧ *crawls off. The PRINCE falls* ⑨ *exhausted on the playboard.*

CASSANDRA: (*entering*) What's the matter, ⑩ Prince Charming? (*The PRINCE* ⑪ *groans.*) Do your feet hurt?

Four dancing couples: A, B, C, D

1. A enters UL, X → UR; B enters DR, X → DL
2. enter UL; dance → UC
3. steps on toes UC
4. groans, limps off UR
5. C enters UR, X → UL; D enters DL, X → DR

6. enter DR; dance DC
7. dip DC; drops her
8. crawls off DR
9. falls DL

10. pop up DR
11. groans

76

PRINCE: (*nodding*) Uh-huh.

12. nods "yes"

CASSANDRA: Aren't the young ladies nice enough?

PRINCE: (*shaking head*) Huh-uh.

13. shakes head "no"

CASSANDRA: Prince, have I got a girl for you! (*Waves wand. CINDERELLA appears on top level.*) Her name is Cinderella.

14. waves wand
15. pops up UC

(*The PRINCE jumps up, looks at CIN-DERELLA, does a double take, and faints.*)

16. jumps up, looks up
17. double take
18. faints DL

CASSANDRA: I thought you'd like her. (*Exits.*)

19. pops down DR

CINDERELLA: (*looking down*) Prince Charming, where are you?

(*The PRINCE jumps up and rushes to the upper level. He bows to CINDERELLA. She curtsies. They dance, ending on the lower level. At the end of the dance, they both bow to each other again.*)

20. gets up; exits DL; enters UL
21. bows
22. curtsies
23. dance out UL; enter DL
    X → DC
24. bow

CINDERELLA: This has been the most beautiful night in my life. Thank you, Prince Charming. (*She gives him a small kiss on the cheek. He faints. The clock starts to strike twelve.*) Oh, dear! (*Shaking him*) Wake up, Prince Charming. (*Picks him up*) I must leave. (*Shakes him again*) Wake up! Sorry, (*drops him*) I just have to go! (*Rushes off.*)

25. kisses him on cheek

26. faints

SD1 clock

27. shakes him

28. picks him up
29. shakes him
30. drops him
31. exits UR

(The PRINCE ³² wakes up and looks around for

CINDERELLA. He ³³ rushes to the top level,

³⁴ sees her slipper, ³⁵ picks it up, and ³⁶ stands look-

ing at it as the lights slowly dim.)

32. gets up, looks around
33. rushes out DL and enters UL
34. sees slipper
35. picks it up
36. looks at it

ACT II, Scene 2

SETTING: *Same as Act I, Scene 1.*

MUSIC: *trumpet fanfare*

Once more the PAGE ¹ enters on horseback,
carrying a trumpet in his downstage hand.

PAGE: ² Hear ye! Hear ye! Prince Charming
is looking for the lady who lost her slipper at

the ball. Whomever it fits will become his

bride. ³ Hear ye! Hear ye! (*Exits, his voice fad-*
ing into the distance as lights fade.)

1. enters UR; speaks as Xs → UC
2. stops; turns DC
3. exits UL

Act II, Scene 3: Page shows glass slipper to Brunhilda. Prince looks at scene from above on Horse.

ACT II, Scene 3

SETTING: *Same as Act I, Scene 3. As the lights come up on the garden, the PRINCE,* ① *on horseback, enters on the upper level. He is* ② *followed by a PAGE carrying a pillow on which rests the glass slipper. The PAGE* ③ *descends to the lower level, leaving the* ④ *PRINCE watching from above.*

1. enters UR; Xs UL; stops
2. enters UR; Xs UL; exits UL
3. enters DL
4. UL

⑤ *GRETCHEN and BRUNHILDA rush on, pushing and pulling, each wanting to be first.*

5. enter R

⑥ BRUNHILDA: That's my slipper!

6. pulling at GR, trying to hold her back

⑦ GRETCHEN: No, it's mine!

7. giving BR a shove backward

⑧ PAGE: Ladies, ladies! One at a time, please!

8. Xing R → them

⑨ ⑩ GRETCHEN: I'm first! (*She pushes and grunts, twists and turns, as she tries to fit her foot into the slipper.*)

9. sits R, back to audience; PAGE kneels facing GR
10. foot business

⑪ PAGE: Sorry, m'lady. Your foot just won't fit into the slipper.

11. gets up; bows

⑫ GRETCHEN: (*assuming a grand manner*) I didn't want to marry the Prince anyway! (*Exits.*)

12. jumps up; nose-in-air exit DR

13. giving GR a shove as she goes by

⑬ BRUNHILDA: Of course it didn't fit her. ⑭ ⑮ The slipper belongs to me! (*She groans and shoves and jumps up and down, trying to force her foot into the shoe.*)

14. sits R, back to audience; PAGE kneels facing BR
15. foot business

16. gets up; bows

⑯ PAGE: It does not fit you either, m'lady!

BRUNHILDA: (*haughtily*) It doesn't matter. (17) I didn't want to live in the palace anyway. They never have enough dessert. (*Exits.*) (18)

17. jumps up; Xs with nose-in-air → R

18. turns back; delivers line; exits DR

PAGE: (*looking up at PRINCE*) I'm sorry, (19) your Highness. They were the last two ladies in the kingdom.

19. bows to PRINCE

(*PAGE, carrying the pillow, exits. As* (20) *PRINCE starts to leave, CASSANDRA* (21) *appears.*)

20. DL

21. starts to exit UL

CASSANDRA: Stop! There is one young lady (22) left. Go down into the garden and wait.

22. pops up UR

(*PRINCE rides off and enters immediately on* (23) *foot in the garden below.*)

23. exits UL; enters DL

CASSANDRA: Where are you, Cinderella? (24)

24. waving wand

CINDERELLA: (*enters wearing old dress*) (25) Prince Charming!

25. enters DR

PRINCE: (*not recognizing her*) Huh? (26)

26. looks her up and down

CASSANDRA: (*waving her wand*) (27) (28) Abra-ca-dabra, feather and fess. (29) Magic and moonlight, (30) Make me a dress!

27. waving wand
28. taps once
29. taps once
30. taps once

(*There is a flash of light. CINDERELLA* (31) (32) *appears, dressed as she was for the ball.*)

31. light flash

32. CIN in old dress is taken down; CIN in ball gown pops up in same place

PRINCE: (*gasps for joy*) Cinderella! (*Faints.*) (33)

33. faints C

CINDERELLA: Oh, no...(*tries to revive* (34)

34. rushes to him; shakes him

him)...not again! (*Tries once more; finally picks him up and slings him over her shoulder.*) Come on, Prince. You'll be late for our wedding.

(*CASSANDRA waves her wand and the pumpkin coach rises out of the vines. CINDERELLA puts the PRINCE in the coach and gets in herself. The BIRD flies on, gets into the harness, and pulls the coach off. The music begins to build. A large pair of wings appear behind CASSANDRA. She flies off. The BIRD returns, carrying a sign that says THE END. It places the sign on the corn-stalk and flies away.*)

35. shakes him again

36. picks him up on shoulder

37. waves wand; coach appears

38. puts PRINCE in coach; gets in herself

39. BIRD enters L; gets into harness

40. exits L
    SD1 music
41. wings come up behind CAS
42. exits UL
43. BIRD enters L with sign

44. puts sign on stalk; exits L

Last scene: Cassandra has earned her wings, as the END sign comes on.

81

Chapter

8

The Rehearsal Schedule and Videotape

For a successful performance, a rehearsal schedule should be established and adhered to. The puppeteers are responsible for memorizing their lines, rehearsing manipulation, and thinking of improvements in characterization of the puppets.

At the beginning of each rehearsal, it is important that you spend a short amount of time checking on the various members' responsibilities and asking them to report on their progress. This establishes channels of communication between you and the group.

In addition to the puppeteers rehearsing their parts, you should schedule rehearsals of the technical crew. This should include lights, sound, moving stage scenery, and working the stage curtains.

There is also the job of un-packing puppets and props, examining them for damage, and setting them on tables or racks backstage. For greater efficiency, you should divide the puppeteers into pairs and assign each pair to work either the right or left side of the stage.

With the aid of a complete checklist, the puppeteers should rehearse placing puppets and props on the proper side of the stage. At the end of the day's rehearsal, the same puppeteers should pack the puppets and props according to the pre-planned diagrams. This will save space and provide for orderly access.

Physical and vocal exercises should be conducted before each rehearsal. These exercises can be practiced at home.

Using a mirror during rehearsal is not recommended for a number of reasons. First, a

In a classroom situation, children love videotapes because they love to see themselves. Make arrangements with the audio-visual instructor to make the equipment available to you. However, use it sparingly since indiscriminate use of a videotape can take time away from rehearsals, becoming a distraction rather than a productive aid.

REHEARSAL SCHEDULE AFTER CASTING

The following sample schedule is based upon a ten-week rehearsal period, four hours per week.

Each member of the group should have a cassette of the sound track and know the incidental music to be used while changing scenes.

mirror cannot substitute for a director or videotape. Second, the mirror would present the performance backwards. Third, if working through a scrim, the mirror would not be seen without considerable distortion.

VIDEOTAPE

The relatively low cost of videotape can make its use of great aid to you. A portable videotape recorder can monitor the progress of the show and provide a check on the quality of manipulation. While the videotape does not take the place of the director, it can help settle differences. For example, are the puppets too high or too low? Is anyone's hand showing? Video is not only an impartial observer, but it also provides a record that can be replayed as often as necessary to improve a performance.

If telephoning members regarding a change of rehearsal time is too big a job for one person, you may wish to set up a telephone committee.

Week	First Hour	Second Hour	Third Hour	Fourth Hour
1	Discuss business. Set dates. Set rehearsal time. Choose telephone crew.	Read through play. Puppeteers reading their parts. Discuss play in detail.	Divide play into three parts. Subdivide into seven sections, called scenes.	Discuss design of play. Show different types of design. Decide on color scheme. Allocate jobs for making puppets, props, costumes, etc.
2	Learn finger manipulation.	Read through Scene 1.	Block Scene 1 with puppeteers without puppets.	Make work puppets.
3	Learn wrist manipulation. Review finger movements.	Review Scene 1 with work puppets.	Block Scene 2 with work puppets.	Make work props.
4	Learn arm manipulation. Review finger and wrist movements.	Review Scene 2 with work puppets. Add to Scene 1.	Block Scene 3.	Start work on good puppet heads, props, and scenery.
5	Improvise pantomime scenes based on play.	Review Scene 3. Add to Scenes 1 and 2.	Block Scene 4.	Keep working on puppets, props, and scenery.
6	Work on puppet voices.	Review Scene 4. Add to Scenes 1, 2, and 3.	Block Scene 5.	Start costumes and wigs. Keep working on puppets, props, and scenery.
7	Start technical discussions.	Review Scene 5. Add to Scenes 1, 2, 3, and 4.	Block Scene 6.	Continue to work on costumes, wigs, puppets, props, etc.
8	Start rehearsing with tech crew.	Review Scene 6. Add to Scenes 1, 2, 3, 4, and 5.	Block Scene 7.	Finish all work on puppets, props, scenery, costumes, etc.
9	Run through tech rehearsal, Scenes 1-7.	Review Scene 7. Add to Scenes 1, 2, 3, 4, 5, and 6.	First run-through with good puppets.	Second run-through with good puppets, scenery, props.
10	Run through entire production.	Run through entire production.	First dress rehearsal.	Second dress rehearsal.

Diagram 9: Rehearsal schedule (10 weeks, 4 hours per week)

Chapter

9

The Performance

Before each performance, make sure the group is briefed. This means the entire cast must know the location and time schedule for the performance. If necessary, include driving instructions. See sample performance schedule.

Know how long it takes to set up and strike set. Observe how equipment is unpacked so that it can be repacked the same way.

A dressing room should be provided for the puppeteers.

Check the entrances and exits on the stage and make sure that everyone knows where they are.

Allow time for meals. Know beforehand what eating facilities are available. Encourage the members of the group to bring snacks if more than one show will be performed.

Something usually goes wrong, so allow time for the unexpected. If something major does in fact go wrong, don't panic. A well-rehearsed group will be able to improvise to cover a fluff. Sometimes, improvising around an error leads to a permanent change in the production.

You, the director, should watch the performance from the audience, not from backstage. This permits you to see the production and to take notes on the performance. Discuss these notes with the group as soon as possible after the performance. If more than one performance is being given in a single day, discuss the comments between shows. If it is necessary to strike set immediately, meet with the group after the return trip. But by all means go over mistakes before

All performers and stage hands should wear black shirts, pants, gloves, and, frequently, hoods. This is necessary because if any part of them is visible to the audience, they will blend into the background. Make sure clothing has no reflective buttons, buckles, or snaps. All stitching on the garments should be in black thread.

the next performance.

The group should also analyze its performance. Perhaps most difficult to analyze is a mediocre performance. Most often, however, what is needed is simply the energy or drive to overcome the slump.

Another difficulty is dealing with staleness in a production that has had a long run. This is common with small groups that use the same show over and over again. It may also happen more frequently with a taped show. Use improvisation to counteract rote delivery of lines and mechanical movement.

Make the puppeteers aware of whatever the problems are so that they can view these problems as a challenge to their creativity and as something that will build their professionalism. Call a rehearsal in the middle of a long run to refresh and tighten the show.

In rating the performance, remember the audience reaction may not be the most objective gauge of how the group performed. You should have your own opinion of how well or poorly the group did.

After a good performance, compliment the group. Encouragement is essential. The group should always feel that you are fair and have confidence in its ability.

When playing for children, put a line of masking tape on the floor in front of the puppet stage. Ask the audience not to cross this line.

CHECKLIST

The following is a checklist of the necessary equipment for a puppet performance. Keep this check list in the production book.

Stage
All sections of stage
Curtains
Curtain rods
Playing board(s)
Hardware
Sand bags
Medium-size step ladder

Lights
Light bars
Light bulbs (3 extras)
Gelatines
Work lights
Hardware
Light box, dimmers
Extension cords
Flashlights
Light clamps
Electrical tape

Sound Equipment
Tape recorder(s)
Amplifier
Speakers
Cassettes or tapes
Connecting cables

Puppets
List of puppets
Packing diagrams

Props and Scenery
List of props
List of scenery
Packing diagrams

Tool Chest
Tools: hammer, screw-drivers, pliers, scissors, ruler, pen, pencils, sandpaper, file, X-ACTO knives
Staple gun and staples
Regular glue (hot glue and cartridges optional)
Extra hardware, hinges, nuts and bolts, nails (different sizes), thumbtacks, screws (machine and wood)

First Aid Kit
Bandages, Band-Aids, antiseptic, sanitary napkins
Aspirin or equivalent
Antacids or equivalent
Cough drops and/or lozenges
Special medication (for special students)

Sewing Kit
Thread to match puppet costumes, plus black and white
Buttons
Snaps
Needles, pins, safety pins
Travelling iron
Carbona or other cleaning fluid

Food Kit

Thermos of hot water
Cups and spoons
Soup, tea, coffee, sugar, bouillon (all packaged)
Fruit juice

Paint Kit

Brushes
Small jars of paints used in production
Set of magic markers
Rags to wipe brushes, etc.

Clothes

Black gloves and hoods
Extra black socks
Extra black top (large size)

Performance Contract

Travelling Directions and Map of Area

List of Work Assignments of Group Members

One copy of the packing diagram for puppets and props should be pasted inside the lid of the appropriate packing case. Another copy of the diagram should be included in the production book.

Information on Group Members

List of names, addresses, and telephone numbers of cast and family
Where applicable, member's medical information and physician's telephone number

Diagram of How to Pack Van (if Travelling)

Extra Set of Car Keys (if Travelling)

Date	Organization and Address of Performance	Setup Time	Performance Time	Departure Location and Time	Miscellaneous

Diagram 10: Performance schedule

Appendix

PUPPET ORGANIZATIONS

Puppeteers of America, Inc.
Gale Schluter, Membership Officer
5 Cricklewood Path
Pasadena, CA 91107

UNIMA-USA
The American Center for the
Union Internationale de la
Marionnette
Allelu Kurten, General Secretary
Browning Road
Hyde Park, NY 12538

THEATRICAL SUPPLY HOUSES

Fabrics
Dazians, Inc.
423 West 55 Street
New York, NY 10019
(212) 307-7800

Felt
Central Shippee, Inc.
Bloomingdale, New Jersey 07403
(800) 631-8968

Lights
Roscolene Swatch Book
Rosco Laboratories
Harrison, NY 10528

Stroblite Company
430 West 14 Street
Room 507
New York, NY 10014
(212) 929-3778

Sound Records
Thomas J. Valentine
Major Records
151 West 46 Street
New York, NY 10036
(212) 869-5210

General Supplies
Theatre House, Inc.
P. O. Box 2090
400 West 3 Street
Covington, KY 41012,
(606) 431-2414

Select Bibliography

The books and pamphlets listed below are available from the Puppetry Store, c/o Rich Morse, 2518 Mountain Ave., Flint, MI 48503. The Store is a division of the non-profit national organization, The Puppeteers of America.

THE ART OF PUPPETRY

Lasky, Kathryn. *Puppeteer.* New York: The MacMillan Company, 1965.

Latshaw, George. *Puppetry, The Ultimate Disguise.* New York: Richards Rosen Press, 1978.

Wright, John. *Rod, Shadow and Glove. Puppets from the Little Angel Theatre.* London: Robert Hale, Ltd., 1986.

HISTORY

Baird, Bil. *The Art of the Puppet.* New York: Collier-MacMillan Company, 1965.

Chesse, Ralph. *The Marionette Actor.* Fairfax, VA: George Mason University Press, 1987.

Leach, Robert. *The Punch and Judy Show—History, Tradition, Meaning.* London: Batsford Academic and Educational Ltd., 1985.

McPharlin, Paul, and Marjorie Batchelder McPharlin. *The Puppet Theatre in America.* Boston: Plays, Inc., 1969.

Obraztsov, Sergei. *My Profession.* Moscow: Foreign Languages Publishing House, 1950.

Philpott, A. R. *Dictionary of Puppetry.* Boston: Plays, Inc., 1969.

MANIPULATION

Engler, Larry, and Carol Fijan. *Making Puppets Come Alive.* New York: Taplinger Publishing Company, 1973.

Schubert, Lettie Connell. *A Manual of Hand Puppet Manipulation.* Self-published: 1980. To order, write to Puppet Images and Books, 14 Eton Way, Mill Valley, CA 94941.

CONSTRUCTION

Devet, Donald, and Drew Allison. *The Wit and Wisdom of Polyfoam Puppet Construction.* Charlotte, NC: Grey Seal Productions, 1983.

Flower, Cedric, and Alan Fortney. *Puppets: Methods and Materials.* Worchester: MA: Davis Publications, 1986.

Scholz, Claire E. *Some Puppet Patterns and Stuff.* Spearfish, SD: Dragons Are Too Seldom, 1981.

Siven, Carole. *Mask Making.* Worchester, MA: Davis Publications, 1986.

PRODUCING/DIRECTING

Coad, Luman, and Arlyn Coad. *Producing for the Puppet Theatre.* Vancouver: Charlemagne Press, 1987.

Fiske, Pat, and James Spearly. *Curtain Calls: Puppetry for Seniors.* Austin, TX: Hogg Foundation, 1980.

Green, Joann. *The Small Theatre Handbook / A Guide to Management and Production.* Boston: The Harvard Common Press, 1981.

RELIGIOUS

Harp, Grace. *Handbook of Christian Puppetry.* Denver: Accent Books, 1984.

Sylwester, Roland. *Teaching Bible Stories More Effectively.* St. Louis: Concordia Publications, 1976.

MISCELLANEOUS

Drossol, Monoa. *Stage Fright—Health and Safety in the Theater.* New York: The Center for Occupational Hazards, Inc., 1986.

Hoggett, Chris. *Stage Crafts.* New York: St. Martin's Press, 1976.

Knesel, Dave. *Free Publicity.* New York: Sterling Publishing Company, 1982.

Korty, Carol. *Writing Your Own Plays.* New York: Scribners, 1986.

Maas, Jane. *Better Brochures, Catalogs, and Mailing Pieces.* New York: St. Martins's Press, 1981.

Mahlmann, Louis, and Leonard Suib. *Music for the Puppet Theatre.* Mineola, NY: Dover Publications, Inc., 1988.

Reiniger, Lotte. *Shadow Theatre and Shadow Films.* New York: Watson-Guptill, 1970.

Ritchard, Dan. *Ventriloquism for the Total Dummy.* New York: Villard Books, 1987.

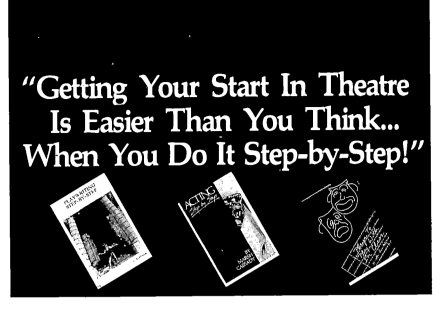